Two of a Kind

by BEATRIZ DOUMERC AND RICARDO ALCANTARA
translated by LAURA M. PEREZ AND KATHRYN CORBETT
illustrations by JACKIE SNIDER

HARCOURT BRACE & COMPANY

Orlando   Atlanta   Austin   Boston   San Francisco   Chicago   Dallas   New York
Toronto   London

Illustrations by Jackie Snider
Illustrations copyright © 1994 by Harcourt Brace and Company

This edition is published by special arrangement with Ediciones Destino, S.A.

English translation copyright © 1994 by Harcourt Brace & Company

Grateful acknowledgment is made to Ediciones Destino, S.A., Barcelona, Spain, for permission to reprint *Two of a Kind* by Beatriz Doumerc and Ricardo Alcántara. Text © 1987 by Ediciones Destino, S.A. Text © by Beatriz Doumerc and Ricardo Alcántara. Originally published in Spain under the title *Tal Para Cual*.

Printed in the United States of America

ISBN 0-15-302202-7

1 2 3 4 5 6 7 8 9 10   011   97 96 95 94 93

It

was exactly 7:10 in the morning when the cat, after a night on the prowl, settled down for a nap in the shade of some shrubs. But he couldn't get to sleep because of a terrible racket coming from the barnyard! Whatever was going on? In two leaps he was at the gate to find out.

It seemed that a hen had just arrived—a hen that had never been seen before. It was as if she had fallen from the sky! Her feathers were patchy and her crest was faded, but one thing was certain: she had an air of importance.

She had come from very far away, she said, and she felt completely exhausted.

"Ah...You can't imagine how much traveling I've done."

"You don't say! And what are you doing strutting

around here?" the nanny goat asked curiously.

The hen gave a little jump back and fluffed up her feathers:

"I'm a storyteller! What I do is tell the romantic tale of Catalina Feather-Tail! Would you like to hear it? I can tell you the story right now complete with feathers and flaps."

"Do we have a choice?" asked the cat, yawning.

"Is it a true story or make-believe?" asked the duck.

"It's all true! Every story I tell is the absolute truth," said the hen.

"Did you know her personally, this Catalina?" asked the dog, shyly.

The hen shuffled her feet and started to stutter:

"No, no. Ev...ev...everything I know about Catalina Feather...Feather-Tail I've been told secondhand. And I tell the story just the way it was told to me!"

"Well, go ahead and get started," said the cat. (He had one eye open and the other one closed.)

"But I need some music to go along with the story!" said the hen, looking all around her.

3

"What are you talking about? This isn't a TV studio. We can't provide background music!" replied the cat.

"Croak, croak, croak…," sang a little frog from his small puddle of water. "I'll do my part… croak, croak, croak…"

"Just a moment," added the dog, and he sprinted off. In a few minutes he came back with a rattle. It was old and rickety, but it could still shake out a tune: *Traca, traca, traca, tracata.*

"Musical accompaniment by a frog and a rattle…," said the hen. "This isn't what I'm used to, but it will have to do. Music, please!"

The audience got comfortable, and the hen began her tale, to the croak-and-rattle beat.

Listen well to my tale,
For the story is true
Of a long-ago school
And a young hen I knew.
A songstress was she
Of innocent heart;
With voice pure and sweet

4

In a show she took part.
But to her dismay,
A scoundrel I'll mention
Spoiled her performance
With wicked intention!

Croak! Trac, trac! Croak! Tracatrac!

The hen had barely finished the first part of her story when they all heard the slam of the barnyard gate. Unbelievable! There stood an old, moth-eaten fox and in the plain light of day!

"Don't be afraid," said the unexpected visitor. "I was just passing by when I heard these beautiful verses. I love to listen to stories, too. If you don't mind, I'll just sit in a corner and listen with all due respect…"

"Oh, no!" everyone protested. "Who knows what you've got hidden up your sleeve!"

"Nothing, I promise! I only want to listen to this clever lady tell her tales. Don't be afraid… Look! My teeth aren't even sharp anymore; my tail is all moth-eaten. And I'm so near-sighted that I

can barely make you out. Ha, ha, ha… I'm not the same fox I used to be!"

The hen, who had been watching him closely, murmured:

"Yes, yes… He's not what he used to be…"

The fox went and sat down in a far-off corner, but everyone kept an eye on him suspiciously. The dog barked, and the cat bared his claws.

"Let him be," said the hen. "I think it would do the gentleman good to hear what I have to say." And without giving any more importance to the matter, she continued:

Well then, as I was saying… I had heard that Catalina Feather-Tail was beautiful and intelligent and that from the time she was little, she had stood out from her playmates. She was studious and hard-working, but of all of her talents, her singing was the greatest. Her voice was marvelous! At all hours of the day, and sometimes even into the night, she pierced the air with her resounding and vibrant "Cocorocooo," which delighted everyone around. Catalina's dream was to be a famous singer.

7

Soon an opportunity came along to show off her talents. In honor of the Patron Saint's Day, great festivities were being planned at school. There were going to be recitals and speeches, dances and plays. And as a grand finale, a debut performance by Catalina of "The Aria for Fowl."

On the appointed day, her parents and teachers were anxiously awaiting her debut from their front-row seats. Behind them were seated all of her classmates. All of them, that is, except one. But this didn't matter to Catalina, because the one that was missing was the worst student at school: a liar and a cheat, greedy and lazy, a cunning trickster and practical joker. A true fox, he was, capable of anything. And of course, while the party was going on, this sinister character was up to no good.

Once the speeches and dances were over, it was finally time for Catalina's performance. The curtain opened, and our beautiful little songstress made her appearance. There were "Hoorays" and lots of clapping. Then a silence so profound came over the audience that the faint buzzing of a fly could be heard. Catalina took a deep breath—she puffed out her chest, stretched her wings, opened her beak, and...a horrible, out-of-tune "Quiquiriqui!" resounded through the theater.

Dear friends, the wicked fox, with a voice like a hoarse old rooster, had cackled out "Quiquiriqui" just at the moment that Catalina had opened her beak. What perfect timing! At first, no one knew what to do. Then some began to laugh, others to whistle, and still others to shout "Quiet!" And from all the far corners of the room, you could hear various versions of "Quiquiriqui!"

The little songstress tried to go on, but there was so much confusion and noise that no one paid any attention to her. Sad and crestfallen, she hid behind the curtain. Her heart was broken into little pieces. She, who had never done anyone any harm!

With these words, the little hen's voice started to tremble, and she couldn't go on. Her audience waited, silent and courteous. Finally, the goat asked, "And what happened to Catalina?"

"She never sang again! Because of that nasty scoundrel, a brilliant career was ruined, and the world lost a great singer! Yes, dear friends, because of the shock she had received, Catalina lost her singing voice forever!"

"What good luck!" murmured the fox from his corner. Everyone turned to look at him.

"What did you say?" they asked in disbelief.

"Nothing, nothing. I said I was lucky to have heard this story," the fox hurried to reply. And, taking three steps forward, he added, "And if you will permit me, I, too, have a story to tell about this 'songstress'."

The hen shook the few feathers she had and stumbled over her feet.

"Don't be nervous, lovely lady!" said the fox with a bow. "What a coincidence! It so happens that in my long-lost youth I knew this Catalina. Personally, that is, not just secondhand, like you. So you see, I have a lot to tell."

"Tell us! Tell us!" shouted everyone.

"Very well. Since this worthy audience requests it... Music, please!"

The frog and the dog with the rattle took their places. The fox, addressing himself to the hen, began to chant:

> The tale you have told
> With such true devotion
> Deserves our respect

For your deep emotion.
But now I will tell
My side of the story
And for this performance
Ask no fame or glory.
I've waited to tell it
For many a season;
And with my good memory
You'll soon see the reason.

Croak! Tracatrac! Croak! Trac, trac!
    To the beat of the frog's croaking and the dog's rattle, our narrator went on:

    Far be it from me to brag, but even as a small child, I astonished one and all with my great knowledge and my warm friendliness. You should have seen how my playmates and teachers looked up to me. Yes, I was the center of attention... until Catalina Feather-Tail showed up at my school. She was so conceited and such a teacher's pet. On the surface she was dripping with smiles, but underneath she was always plotting mean tricks. And I was the one she always picked on. She cut me down with nasty remarks and stole the punch lines of my jokes. She stuck signs on my back, she took my lunch, and she hid my notebooks. And I, who always had such a nice disposition, never said anything. But inside I was burning up like a volcano! One time, fed up with her dirty tricks, I exclaimed:

"How hateful you are! I can't stand to look at you!"

The teacher happened to pass by just at that moment. "What did you say?" she asked.

"I said that I can't see Catalina," I answered quickly.

"But she's sitting right next to you!"

"Maybe so, but I still can't see her."

"You must need glasses," said the teacher. "I'll be sure to tell your mother."

"Jacinto needs glasses?" my mother said worriedly. That very afternoon she decided to take me to the eye doctor. I didn't want to go, but there was nothing I could do about it.

We were on the way to the eye doctor's office when suddenly I got an idea: Nobody at school wore glasses. If I wore

glasses, I'd be the only one who had them. They would make me even more popular than Catalina Feather-Tail!

It was a clever idea, and I put it right to work.

"What letter is this on the chart?" asked the eye doctor.

"What chart?" I asked.

"The one on the wall here," he said, pointing to it.

"What wall?" I asked, with an air of innocence.

"Oh, my! There's no doubt you need glasses!" exclaimed the eye doctor.

He prescribed glasses for me that were so strong I couldn't see anything at all. But this didn't matter. The next day, I arrived at school glowing with happiness. From far away, I could see that something was going on. My school friends had formed a ring... Around whom? "Surely it must be a ring around Catalina," I thought. I groped my way towards them, wearing my brand-new glasses. Ah, what I saw so blurrily and heard so clearly made me shake with anger! There was Catalina Feather-Tail strutting around with three pairs of glasses hanging from her neck!

"These are for seeing things that are far away," she explained. "And these are for things that are close up, and these are for the sun..." Everyone was dazzled!

14

Humiliated all the way down to the tip of my tail, I put my glasses away in a hurry so that no one would notice them. I only had one pair of glasses—she had three!

"Three!" repeated the fox, holding up his paw.

"That hen sure got away with a lot," observed the cat.

"Three pairs of glasses… Just to show off, of course!" said the duck.

"Ah, dear friends, I assure you that ever since that day, I have never touched those glasses again," explained the fox. "Even though I desperately need glasses now, I refuse to wear them. Because of that, I can barely make you out now."

"We're better off that way," said the hen in a low voice. And raising her crest, she commanded:

"Music, please!"

Everyone settled down to listen to her. She cleared her throat and began to tell her story to the beat of the music.

The tale I have told
Is truly no lie.

It's only the truth
I'm inspired by.
But I'm well aware
That the saying is true:
We color our world
By the lens we look through.
I won't waste your time
If you lend me your ears;
Here's more of that story
Of long-ago years.

Even though she had lost her wonderful voice, Catalina went on through school, always earning the highest grades. When she had grown up, she still loved the arts more than anything else. Day after day she asked herself, "What can I do, since I'm not able to sing?"

Then she thought of an answer: "If I can't sing, I'll learn to dance." She immediately began to practice some dance steps.

It took a very long time, but she finally became an expert dancer. She performed on many stages and was always a great success.

Now, I have to tell you about Catalina's tail. It was thick and multicolored and it fluttered like a fan. Its colors glowed under the stage lights. It was a thing of beauty—how it rippled and fluttered to the beat of the music! It was her best feature.

One day, her agent, the famous Herculano, suggested to her:

"Catalina, you ought to buy insurance for your tail."

"Oh! Do you think so?" asked Catalina, surprised.

"Of course. Next week we'll take care of it," said Herculano.

Next week! What a grave mistake they made in not insuring that valuable tail that instant! The next day, the unexpected happened. A strange character came to the theater and asked to see Herculano in private. The stranger claimed he was an internationally famous magician, and he had newspapers and magazines in every language to prove it. He was The Great Perengano! He wore a roomy cape and a top hat, he twirled his baton like a whirlwind, and… his face was covered with a black mask!

"It's part of my costume," he said, grinning. Behind the mask, his eyes were shining like bright, red-hot coals.

He performed two or three magic tricks, and Herculano signed him up right then and there. That very night he made his

19

debut and was a huge success. When he finished his act, the audience applauded enthusiastically: "Bravo! Encore! More!" they shouted from every corner of the theater.

"Do another trick for them," said Herculano, hidden behind the curtain.

"I have a sensational number," the magician told him, "but I would need an assistant. If our lovely little dancer would like to help me out…"

"Of course I will," Catalina hastened to say, helpful and polite as always.

When the two of them appeared before the expectant audience, The Great Perengano pointed to a trunk that he had placed in the center of the stage and announced, "Next, I shall perform for you a trick that has never before been seen by the human eye: The Relentless Handsaw!" To Catalina, he said politely, "Please step into the trunk." She did so, and the magician continued:

"Now, I will close the lid of the trunk, and I will saw the trunk in half, from side to side."

The audience shuddered, and so did Catalina. The Great Perengano whispered to her, "You have nothing to be afraid of, my dear. It's only a magic trick."

The lid was shut, and Catalina was in total darkness.
Suddenly…Rash, rash, rash! Catalina wanted to cry out a
"Cocorocooooo!" for help, but now she had completely lost her voice.
The beautiful plumes of her feathered tail fell, one by one, to the
bottom of the trunk.

Then the lid of the trunk was raised, and Catalina heard The
Great Perengano's voice saying, "Observe! I have cut the trunk
completely in half, and our little ballerina is still in one piece. She's lost
only a few little feathers from her tail."

A few feathers! Catalina was ruined! Up until then, she hadn't
realized who Perengano really was…her long-time enemy, the fox!

Ah, dear friends! Because of this terrible scoundrel, Catalina
Feather-Tail's career was smashed to pieces again, and the world had
lost one of its greatest dancers.

"What a shame!" said the goat, thoughtfully.

"A victim of foxiness," said the duck. And everyone looked
at the fox. But the fox wasn't at all concerned. He motioned to the
frog and the dog to start up the music, and began to chant:

I have listened in silence
And tell you now still,
You will not confuse me
With tale-spinning skill.
I have a big heart—
I'd hold out a hand
To help my worst enemy
In all the land.
Throughout my whole life—
Unlike some I could mention—
I've shown only kindness
And all good intention.

Yes, ladies and gentlemen, kindness and good intention! On that long-ago occasion, upon seeing Catalina Feather-Tail with her ruined tail, I felt just terrible. Never, I repeat, never had it crossed my mind to bring her to such a state. It was a horrible accident, a trick of fate. All the same, I felt as if it were my fault. My heart swelled up in my chest.

Here's what I did: with tears in my eyes (and that's the truth!), I went to speak with Herculano. I wanted to find some way to fix this disaster.

23

"Catalina could work with me in the hypnotism trick," I suggested.

"No, no," said Herculano, shaking his great head of hair. "Without her splendid tail, Catalina just isn't the same."

"Oh, I agree. Without her colorful tail feathers she's just a common, run-of-the-mill hen. Furthermore, she's knock-kneed and dumpy," I added. "But in order to help me with this trick, she won't need that handful of feathers." I kept talking until, finally, Herculano gave in.

"All right, I'll give her another chance. But will she agree to do it?"

"Yes, I'd be happy to do it," responded Catalina when we asked her. And she stared at me fixedly. Her little eyes were shining as if there were a blowtorch behind each one. And I, sensitive by nature, couldn't help shuddering.

What is going on inside that little head? I wondered. But since I'm overly trusting by nature, I didn't worry about what might happen.

When it was time for the show and The Great Perengano was announced, I came running out with Catalina.

"As our special guest tonight...Catalina Feather-Tail!" said the announcer. A rude member of the audience called out:

"It looks like someone used your tail to make a feather duster!"

Everyone laughed at his joke with big, hearty chuckles. I was so sorry for poor, unfortunate Catalina! But she spread out her feathers—the ones that were left—and went on as if nothing had happened.

"Ladies and gentlemen of the audience," I finally announced, "I shall now hypnotize this hen!"

When I looked at Catalina, I had the uncomfortable feeling that she was trying hard not to laugh. Overlooking this detail, I continued:

"You are getting sleepy… Your eyelids are getting heavy… Your eyes are closing…"

Catalina closed her eyes.

"You will do whatever I tell you to do; right?"

She nodded her head up and down. And I, thinking that everything was going just fine, went on to say:

"You cannot move your body. You can't even open your eyes…You are completely asleep!"

Catalina's eyes flew open. "Do you think so? I don't think so!" she said, shaking her little head back and forth. And spreading her wings wide, off she flew, piercing the air with a shrill "Cocorocoo!" and making me the laughingstock of the show.

"Wh-wh-what? Hadn't she lost her singing voice forever?" asked the dog with a look of amazement on his face.

"Ah, dear listeners! You be the judge. There are those who say that Catalina's losing her voice was purely an act!"

"That's a bold-faced lie!" shouted the hen indignantly.

"Be that as it may," said the fox, paying no attention to her, "the fact of the matter is that Catalina took off flying and cackling." He continued his tale:

"What a fraud!" shouted the audience. "This is a farce! What a joke!"

"I'm ruined!" wailed Herculano, pulling his hair out. "Perengano, you're fired! Get out of here! I don't ever want to set eyes on you again!"

"I left. I didn't have any choice in the matter. Once again I had to hit the streets in search of a job. And whose fault was it?" the fox asked his attentive listeners.

"It was Catalina Feather-Tail's fault!" they all responded at the same time.

"That's right...but I, who have always been as good as gold, I don't hold it against her."

"Just a moment!" shouted the hen, ruffling her feathers. And without waiting for any music, she flew all the way to the top of a tree. From there she called down:

I've never in all my life
Heard such a lie!
And if there's a reason,
I'd like to know why.
I've traveled the world,
Danced for peasant and king;
I've worked for my living,
Not asked for a thing.
So your lying stories
Will not disturb me.
No one has been born
Who can stop me—you'll see!

Croak! Tracatrac! Croak! Trac, trac!

The dog and the frog hurried to start the music, and the hen went on:

With her brilliant career as a dancer so cruelly ended, Catalina asked herself once again, "What shall I do?" One night, she found the answer: "If I can't sing or dance, why don't I specialize in flying?"

Yes, dear friends, Catalina Feather-Tail became a flyer. Ah, but I already know what you're thinking: "A hen that flies isn't anything out of the ordinary." But Catalina's flights were completely different from those of any common hen! They were acrobatic flights! This was a skill that she achieved only after much practice. She would fly up like a whirlwind, and then she'd dive straight down at a dizzying speed. Just before she reached the ground, she'd soar back up with the grace of a butterfly. She would fly figures in the air. Then she would become a leaf blown by the wind, a balloon, a comet, an airplane, a helicopter…always propelled by her wonderful wings!

Her acrobatic flights became the main attraction at a great outdoor show. This was the happiest time ever for Catalina… until a wire crossed her path!

You may say, "A wire…So what? All you have to do is dodge it!" But that's difficult to do when you're hurtling through the air at

supersonic speed! You see, at this moment Catalina was imitating a space shuttle and didn't even see the fateful wire.

It was horrible—a tangle of feathers flying through the air, a broken beak, a torn crest, and bruises all over. And her poor feet—twisted around backwards in the tangles of wire! Who could have put this wire across her flight path? Was it fate? Or was it her eternal enemy, her fateful foe?

The hen flew down from the tree and sat in the middle of the barnyard. Her listeners remained silent. Not one had an answer to the hen's question. Finally the cat dared to say, "Well... I think that the only one who can answer that question..."

"Is I!" interrupted the fox, jumping to his feet. He looked all around at his audience, but he was so near-sighted that he could barely make them out. Even less could he see the hen, who was fluttering up and down the tree.

Seeing that the fox was ready to answer the question, the dog and the frog began their music again, and the story continued:

Who ever would think
That a head so small
Could carry inside it
A tale so tall!
This plot against me,
Without reason or rhyme,
Has left on my heart
A scar for all time.
In a terrible quarrel
I find myself caught.
Here's my story, and you may
Believe it or not.
The end of this tale
You must judge when it's through:
Who's right, fox or hen?
It will be up to you!

I'll tell you another time about the wandering I did for a long time after Herculano fired me. But finally, thanks to my talent and hard work, I became the ringmaster of the Big Bang

Circus. I'm sure you've heard of it. In the Big Bang Circus there are many wonderful performers, but I found myself thinking of Catalina Feather-Tail. What had become of her?

Of course I knew nothing about her accident with the fateful wire. And I was surprised to find that, after not having seen her for so long, I missed her.

So I said to myself, "Jacinto, you need to do everything possible to meet up with her again." So, with only the best intentions, I put an advertisement in the newspaper. It said: "Intelligent hen needed, with artistic talents and a desire to get to the top."

A few hopeful hens showed up, but no Catalina. So I ran the advertisement again. Just when I had given up hope of finding her, she showed up! To tell the truth, she wasn't looking very elegant, shall we say. Her feet were twisted, her feathers were in sad shape, and she was wearing a silly fake tail. But when she asked to speak to the ringmaster,
I welcomed her with open arms and said, "I'm the ringmaster!"

"If you take one more step, you'll be sorry," she threatened me, waving her umbrella.

Can you imagine my disappointment? After such a long time

without seeing each other... What a way to treat me! I still remember how much her words hurt me. But, overcoming my feelings, I told her:

"Catalina, my dear Catalina, let's make our peace..."

"First, we will settle our contract," she answered me, cold and calculating as ever. "I want you to promise me that I will get to the top!"

"Higher than you can possibly imagine!" I promised her. "I'll make you a star!"

"I certainly hope this isn't another of your cunning tricks..."

"Catalina...I swear by our old friendship!" I said to her in a solemn tone of voice.

At this she broke out in a moching laugh...and that very night we signed the contract!

My promises were not false. Catalina did go very high; her number required it! It was the riskiest act in the whole Big Bang Circus. It was called "The Feathered Rocket," and it went like this: Catalina placed herself in the mouth of a small but powerful cannon. I filled it with gunpowder, and then I lit the fuse!

This daring act took place out in the open air; it attracted a crowd of thousands on its opening day. When Catalina appeared on

the platform, the audience clapped enthusiastically. And truly, she looked pretty in her sequined cape and her little gold cap. Everything went just as planned. Wiggling a little bit here and a little bit there, Catalina managed to squeeze herself into the cannon. When she told me she was ready, I loaded up a small charge of gunpowder, lit the fuse, and…BOOOOOOOOMMM!

What a beautiful sight! The Feathered Rocket shot up into the sky, shining like a multicolored comet. Then, braking with her wings, she came in for a smooth landing in the net.

The audience cheered wildly, and our success was repeated for the next several nights. Then Catalina came to me and said, "Tell me, what would happen if you used a double load of gunpowder?"

"Nothing," I answered, "you'd go a little bit higher, but you wouldn't be in any sort of danger."

And I knew exactly what I was talking about. A double charge wasn't dangerous, and it would be the crowning touch on an already daring experiment.

We didn't discuss the matter any further. But that night, when it was time for our act, seeing Catalina so proud and excited, I said to myself: "Why not use the double charge?

Catalina will go even higher, and she'll be so thrilled. What a great surprise!"

And that's what I did, full of good intentions. At the very moment that I lit the fuse, I saw her little head sticking out of the mouth of the cannon, and I whispered to her:

"You're going to go much higher! Much higher! AND..."
BOOOOOOOOMMMMM!

That was the last time that I ever saw Catalina Feather-Tail! I can still remember her little face...

The fox stopped talking. Everyone was waiting, and they all asked at the same time:

"What happened? What then?"

"What happened?!... Nobody ever knew!" answered the fox in a broken voice.

"Nobody ever found out?"

"Nobody ever did. Catalina Feather-Tail was shot out of that cannon like a fireball on its way to the stars...and she never came back!"

"You don't say!" said the cat. "What a dramatic ending!

It makes my fur stand on end and gives me goose bumps!"

"What could have happened?" asked the goat.

Then the hen, flying to the top of the tree, very seriously and gravely announced, "I know the answer."

Everyone became silent, and Catalina Feather-Tail took up the tale:

> The story you've told
> Has moved me to tears,
> So I'll waste no time
> To calm your fears.
> As I finish this tale
> Of mistaken intention,
> I ask you to give me
> Your close attention.
> I don't like to judge
> The deeds of the past,
> But Fate has a way
> Of winning at last!

All of you are asking, "What happened?" I've asked myself the same question, up until this very moment. And now that I have the answer, I'll tell it to you. Think back to the moment when Catalina Feather-Tail asked the fox, "What would happen if you put a double charge in the cannon?"

My dear friends, what made her ask that question? Well, it was something very important. On the first night that she was shot up into the sky, she realized that she was recovering her voice! Yes, night after night, the blast from the cannon made her sing out sweet-sounding "cocorocoos"! But she still hadn't completely gotten back her singing voice. So Catalina Feather-Tail thought: "With a double blast of gunpowder, the blast will be stronger, and I'll get back all of my singing voice. I'll return to singing, my old career!"

And on the fateful night, before the show and without anyone seeing her, she sneaked in and put a charge of gunpowder in the cannon!

"AAAH!" shouted the fox. "Now I understand! She loaded a charge, and I loaded two more!"

"So that means there were three blasts all together," said

the frog, looking frightened.

"Poor Catalina," said the fox. "I wonder what ever happened to her?"

"She went up to outer space!" said the hen. "And there she's orbiting the earth, going around and around. At first, I kept count, but then I lost track. I counted up to 11,897 orbits!"

"And how do you know for sure?" asked the cat, looking at her suspiciously.

A tense hush fell over the barnyard. Suddenly they all started talking at once:

"Yes, how do you know?"

"Who told you?"

"Surely, you made it all up!"

The hen stretched herself. She paused for a few seconds, and then she chanted:

> Quiet down, my dears, please:
> Give me your attention
> So you'll understand

41

The things that I'll mention.
I must tell you the truth:
I am Catalina Feather-Tail!

"You? You're Catalina Feather-Tail!? Well, why didn't you say so before?"

"And how did you get back to Earth?"

"Is what you've told us true?"

And the hen answered:

"It's all true. One day, I began to come down, don't ask me how. Little by little, I started losing speed, until finally I found myself on solid ground. I was in a strange place! So I began to walk. I was old, tired, and airsick. "What shall I do?" I asked myself. And one day I found the answer: "If I can't sing, or dance, or fly as I did before, then I'll devote myself to telling stories. I'll tell the story of Catalina Feather-Tail, my own story! But I'll do it incognito."

"Incognito! But why?" they all asked.

"To free myself from my fateful foe—my eternal enemy, Jacinto Big Ears!"

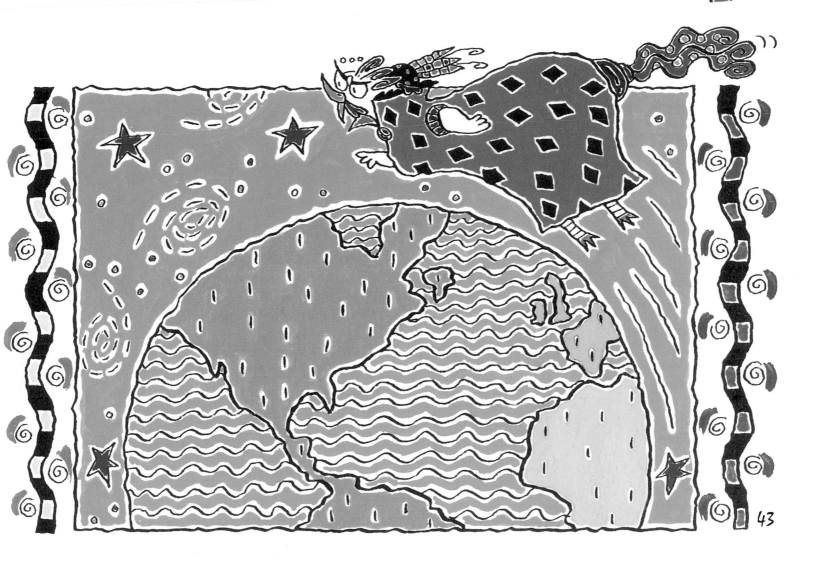

"That's incredible! And now you've found him in this very barnyard," said the goat.

The fox didn't know what to do or what to say. Was he so old, tired, and near-sighted that he hadn't even recognized Catalina? Ah! It was because they had both changed so much. They didn't look at all the same.

Slowly, he walked toward the hen; he got very close and looked at her hard. "Yes, yes, there's no doubt. You are Catalina Feather-Tail! You still have the same sparkle in your eyes!" said the fox in a broken voice.

"Really, Jacinto?" she asked, fluffing her feathers.

The rest of the animals in the barnyard watched them closely. Then they asked, "Now that you've found each other, what do you plan to do?"

The hen and the fox didn't have a thing to say. Then the cat approached them and said, "If you'll allow me… Music, please!" *Croak! Traca, traca, trac! Croak!*

Somewhat surprised, the dog and the frog began the music, and the cat went on to say:

44

This tale is not ended;
Much more is to come.
You two weave a story
That's second to none.
The mind has its wings—
You have nothing to fear;
For better or worse,
You've met again here,
Both looking for something
You're hoping to find.
You must know by now
You are TWO OF A KIND!

Applause broke out in the barnyard.

"Very well said!"

"You're absolutely right!

"Two of a kind! Isn't that the truth!"

By now, it was afternoon and everyone was getting hungry. Listening to the stories had made them forget about everything, even eating.

Catalina Feather-Tail and Jacinto Big Ears were invited to dinner, and they ate hungrily but with very good manners. Afterward, they said their goodbyes and set off together down the road. They had so much to tell each other that they couldn't stop talking.

Then the cat curled up and got ready to take a nap. He thought he should rest awhile. After all, he was going out on the prowl again tonight!